Whiteout!
A Book About Blizzards

by Rick Thomas
illustrated by Denise Shea

Content Adviser: Daniel Dix, Senior Meteorologist,
The Weather Channel

Reading Adviser: Susan Kesselring, M.A., Literacy Educator,
Rosemount-Apple Valley-Eagan (Minnesota) School District

PICTURE WINDOW BOOKS
Minneapolis, Minnesota

Managing Editor:
Catherine Neitge
Creative Director: Terri Foley
Art Director: Keith Griffin
Editor: Patricia Stockland
Designer: Nathan Gassman
Page production: Picture Window Books
The illustrations in this book were
prepared digitally.
Picture Window Books
5115 Excelsior Boulevard
Suite 232
Minneapolis, MN 55416
877-845-8392
www.picturewindowbooks.com

**Library of Congress
Cataloging-in-Publication Data**
Thomas, Rick, 1954-
Whiteout! : a book about blizzards
/ by Rick Thomas ;
illustrated by Denise Shea.
p. cm. — (Amazing science)
Includes bibliographical references
and index.
ISBN 1-4048-0925-2 (hardcover)
1. Blizzards—Juvenile literature.
2. Snow—Juvenile literature. I. Shea,
Denise, ill. II. Title. III. Series.

QC926.37.T48 2004
551.55'5—dc22
2004019738

Table of Contents

Blue-gray clouds creep into the sky. Windows glow in the growing darkness. You are leaving school early. A blizzard is on the way.

It will be a long ride home in the blowing snow.

Whiteout

Driving in a blizzard is very dangerous. Busy windshield wipers keep shoving aside the heavy flakes. Streets and roads are carpeted in thick snow. The snow turns to slush under car tires. The slick slush makes the car slip and slide.

The winds blow harder. More snow falls.
The world becomes a wall of white. Up,
down, sideways—everything looks the
same. The blowing snow has turned into
a blinding whiteout.

Stranded

Whump! The car slides into a soft, thick snowbank. The wheels are stuck. You're stranded by the blizzard.

It's safer to stay in the car than to step outside in the freezing whiteout. Call 911 from a cell phone, or wait for help. Tow trucks, snowplows, and highway troopers are cruising the streets, looking for drivers in trouble.

What's that?
Headlights gleam
faintly through the snow.
A patrol car has stopped to help.

Big and Small Snowflakes

Home at last! Snowflakes keep drifting past your window. Snowflakes fall when the temperature is close to 32 degrees Fahrenheit or lower. The warmer the temperature, the bigger the flakes.

Watch the flakes stream past the light of a streetlight. The flakes are small and powdery. The air is growing colder.

Blizzard!

The next morning, school has been cancelled. The house shudders against the moaning wind. **Woooooooooo!** Windowpanes rattle. Snow blows through the yard in thick, white blasts. The air is so full of snow that you can barely see the houses across the street.

The blizzard is still going strong!

Dangerous Wind and Snow

A blizzard is a fierce combination of wind and snow. Winds blow at more than 35 miles per hour. That's faster than a car on a city street. Snow either showers down from storm clouds or is picked up from the ground by bone-chilling blasts of wind.

Blizzards bring low visibility. That means the blowing snow blocks your vision. In a blizzard, a person can see only as far as 400 yards, or four football fields away.

Sudden gusts of snow block your vision even more. In severe blizzards, people are unable to see their hands in front of their faces.

Snowdrifts

You try to open the back door to let out the dog. The door feels stuck. Outside, the wind has piled up a heavy drift of snow that almost reaches the doorknob.

Television announcers warn that the blizzard could last for several days.

Wind Chill and Frostbite

The thermometer outside shows the temperature is 30 degrees—not terribly cold. But wind blowing against your skin makes cold air feel even colder. That's called wind chill. This morning, with wind gusts of 40 miles per hour, the wind chill is only 13 degrees above zero! When you step outside, you'll feel 17 degrees colder than the thermometer shows.

Frostbite is when temperatures freeze your skin. Hands and ears can turn white. Or you could lose the feeling in your fingers. If you go outside, cover up in layers of warm clothing. Especially cover your fingers, ears, and nose.

Digging Out

The next day, school has been cancelled again. The blizzard is gone, but it has left behind a world of white. It will take a full day to remove snow from streets and driveways. Then school buses can drive safely again.

School is closed, but there is plenty of work to do. The driveway and sidewalks need to be cleared. After that, a snowman can be built. Snowshoes and shovels—and your dog—are waiting for you by the back door.

Surviving a Blizzard

People who attempt to drive in a storm may end up in a crash. More than half the deaths that occur in a blizzard are related to automobiles. Some people become trapped in their cars and ignore simple safety rules. Here's what to do if you are stranded in a car during a blizzard.

- Have the driver run the engine for 10 minutes every hour. This will give you heat.

- Turn on the inside light when the engine is running. The light will help attract attention from passing cars.

- Open a window a tiny bit for fresh air and to prevent carbon monoxide poisoning.

- Make sure the car's exhaust pipe is not covered with snow.

- Move your hands, fingers, and legs around. Keep the warm blood circulating in your body.

- Tie a bright cloth to the car's antenna or door. Open the hood of the car. This will alert passing vehicles that you need help.

Extreme Storm Extras

- The word "blizzard" was first used by German settlers in Iowa. It comes from the German word "blitzartig," which means "like lightning." It describes the deadly speed of the winter winds.

- Most blizzards in North America strike along the "Snowbelt," which stretches from Maine to Minnesota, across the Great Lakes.

- Blizzards also occur in mountain regions. Narrow valleys can suffer winter winds of 100 miles (160 kilometers) per hour.

- Blizzards can cause power outages. Winds and heavy snow can break or blow over power lines. The dangerous loss of power means no heat for hundreds or thousands of households.

- Hypothermia is another danger during winter storms. When exposed to cold, a person's body temperature may drop. Hypothermia means "under-heated." Symptoms of hypothermia are shivering, sluggishness, stumbling, and slurred speech.

Glossary

drifts—piles of snow that are caused by strong winds

frostbite—the condition that happens when skin freezes

slush—a messy mix of snow and water

stranded—trapped or left alone without help

visibility—the ease with which a person can see in certain weather conditions

wind chill—how cold it feels outside measured by the temperature and wind speed; not the same as the actual temperature

To Learn More

At the Library

Chambers, Catherine. *Blizzard*. Chicago: Heinemann Library, 2002.

Turck, Mary C. *Blizzard!: Snowstorm Fury*. Logan, Iowa: Perfection Learning, 2000.

Wright, Betty Ren. *The Blizzard*. New York: Holiday House, 2003.

On the Web

FactHound offers a safe, fun way to find Web sites related to this book. All of the sites on FactHound have been researched by our staff. *www.facthound.com*

1. Visit the FactHound home page.
2. Enter a search word related to this book, or type in this special code: 1404809252
3. Click on the FETCH IT button.

Your trusty FactHound will fetch the best sites for you!

Index

Look for all of the books in this series:

Eye of the Storm: A Book About Hurricanes
Flakes and Flurries: A Book About Snow
Gusts and Gales: A Book About Wind
Nature's Fireworks: A Book About Lightning
Rising Waters: A Book About Floods
Rumble, Boom! A Book About Thunderstorms
Shapes in the Sky: A Book About Clouds
Sizzle! A Book About Heat Waves
Splish! Splash! A Book About Rain
Sunshine: A Book About Sunlight
Twisters: A Book About Tornadoes
Whiteout! A Book About Blizzards